FLIPPING HOUSES 101
A BEGINNER'S GUIDE TO REAL ESTATE PROFITS
BY
WILLIAM JONES
2023

Flipping Houses 101: A Beginner's Guide to Real Estate Profits by William Jones
This edition was created and published by Mamba Press
©MambaPress 2023

Contents

Chapter 1: Introduction to House Flipping
    Chapter 2: Building Your Foundation
    Chapter 3: The Art of Real Estate Analysis
    Chapter 4: Making Deals and Negotiations
    Chapter 5: Funding Your Flips
    Chapter 6: Crafting a Flawless Renovation Plan
    Chapter 7: Executing the Flip
    Chapter 8: Marketing and Selling Your Flip
    Chapter 9: Closing the Deal
    Chapter 10: Learning and Growing
    Chapter 11: Pitfalls to Avoid
    Chapter 12: Case Studies: Real-Life Flipping Examples
    Chapter 13: Beyond Flipping: Long-Term Real Estate Wealth
Appendix

Chapter 1: Introduction to House Flipping

Understanding the Basics: What is House Flipping?

House flipping is a real estate investment strategy where an investor purchases a property with the intent to renovate and resell it for a profit. The goal is to buy properties at a lower price, enhance their value through strategic renovations, and then sell them at a higher price, ideally within a short time frame. Flipping houses requires a combination of market knowledge, financial acumen, project management skills, and a creative eye for design.

The Appeal of House Flipping: Potential Rewards and Challenges

Potential Rewards:

- Profit Potential: Successful flips can yield substantial profits, making it an attractive investment opportunity.
- Active Income: House flipping allows investors to actively engage in the process and see tangible results.
- Real Estate Experience: It can serve as a stepping stone to further real estate ventures or a career in the industry.

Challenges:

- Financial Risks: Flipping involves substantial upfront costs, and there's a risk of overestimating potential profits.
- Time Constraints: Flips require efficient project management to ensure timely completion and sale.
- Market Volatility: Economic fluctuations and changing real estate trends can impact a flip's success.
- Renovation Hurdles: Unexpected issues during renovations can eat into profits.

The House Flipping Process at a Glance

1. **Research and Planning:** Identify your target market, location, and property criteria. Conduct thorough market research to understand property values, demand, and competition.
2. **Financing:** Secure funding through personal savings, loans, partnerships, or private lenders. Create a budget that includes acquisition costs, renovation expenses, and carrying costs.
3. **Property Acquisition:** Source potential properties through real estate agents, auctions, online listings, or off-market deals. Evaluate properties based on location, condition, and potential for value appreciation.
4. **Renovation Strategy:** Develop a detailed renovation plan that outlines the scope of work, timeline, and budget for repairs and upgrades.
5. **Renovation Execution:** Oversee the renovation process, ensuring quality workmanship and adhering to the project timeline.
6. **Marketing:** Create an appealing listing with professional photos and descriptions. Consider staging the property to highlight its potential.
7. **Sale:** Price the property competitively based on market trends and recent comparable sales. Host open houses to attract potential buyers.
8. **Closing:** Once a buyer is secured, navigate the closing process, which involves paperwork, inspections, and legal formalities.
9. **Profit Analysis:** Evaluate the financial outcome of the flip, taking into account all expenses and the final sale price.
10. **Learning and Scaling:** Reflect on the experience, learn from successes and challenges, and consider scaling your house flipping business.

House flipping requires a blend of skills, including financial analysis, property assessment, negotiation, project management, and marketing. As you progress through this guide, you'll gain insights into each stage of the process, equipping you with the knowledge and tools needed to embark on a successful house flipping journey.

Chapter 2: Building Your Foundation

Getting Started: Setting Clear Goals and Expectations

Before diving into the world of house flipping, it's crucial to define your goals and expectations. Consider the following points:

1. **Profit Goals:** Determine how much profit you aim to make from each flip. Research typical profit margins in your chosen market to set realistic expectations.
2. **Time Frame:** Decide how quickly you want to complete each flip. Be aware that longer holding periods increase carrying costs and market risks.
3. **Risk Tolerance:** Assess your willingness to take risks. House flipping involves financial uncertainty and unexpected challenges, so understanding your risk tolerance is essential.
4. **Skill Level:** Evaluate your existing skills and knowledge in areas such as real estate, construction, and project management. Recognize areas where you might need to learn or seek assistance.

Financing Your Flips: Exploring Funding Options

Flipping houses requires upfront capital for property acquisition, renovations, and carrying costs. Explore various funding options:

1. **Personal Savings:** Using your own funds minimizes debt and interest payments but might limit your ability to undertake multiple projects.
2. **Traditional Financing:** Conventional mortgages or loans from banks can offer competitive interest rates, especially if you have a strong credit history.
3. **Private Lenders:** Private individuals or groups can provide funding with potentially more flexible terms than traditional

lenders.
4. **Hard Money Loans:** These short-term loans are secured by the property itself and are a common choice for house flippers due to their quick approval process.
5. **Partnerships:** Joining forces with a financial partner can provide additional capital and expertise, but be sure to outline roles and expectations in a clear agreement.

Developing a Flipping Strategy: Finding Your Niche and Market
Identifying a specific niche and target market can set you up for success:

1. **Property Type:** Decide whether you'll focus on single-family homes, condos, multifamily units, or a mix. Each type has its own advantages and challenges.
2. **Neighborhoods:** Research different neighborhoods to understand property values, market demand, and growth potential. Consider factors like schools, amenities, and proximity to employment centers.
3. **Property Condition:** Determine whether you'll focus on distressed properties that need extensive renovations or properties that require cosmetic upgrades.
4. **Competitive Advantage:** Identify what sets you apart from other flippers. It could be your design aesthetic, efficient project management, or a unique marketing strategy.
5. **Exit Strategy:** Plan what you'll do if a property doesn't sell as quickly as anticipated. Having a backup plan, such as renting or adjusting the sale price, is crucial.

By setting clear goals, securing appropriate funding, and developing a focused strategy, you'll establish a strong foundation for your house flipping endeavors. In the following chapters, we'll delve deeper into the real estate analysis process and guide you through each step of successfully flipping houses for profit.

Chapter 3: The Art of Real Estate Analysis

The Importance of Market Research: Identifying Hot Markets

Effective market research is the cornerstone of successful house flipping. Here's how to identify and evaluate hot markets:

1. **Market Trends:** Study historical and current market trends to understand patterns of property appreciation, demand, and supply.
2. **Economic Indicators:** Monitor economic factors such as job growth, population influx, and development projects that can impact property values.
3. **Neighborhood Analysis:** Evaluate neighborhoods based on crime rates, school quality, proximity to amenities, and overall desirability.
4. **Competition:** Analyze the number of active listings, time properties spend on the market, and the volume of recent sales in a given area.

Finding the Right Properties: Factors to Consider

When selecting properties for flipping, consider these crucial factors:

1. **Location:** A prime location can significantly impact a property's potential for appreciation and resale. Proximity to schools, public transportation, shopping centers, and job hubs matters.
2. **Property Condition:** Assess the property's current state. Is it a cosmetic fixer-upper or a major renovation project? Accurate cost estimation is vital for profitability.
3. **Comparable Sales:** Research recent sales of similar properties in the area to gauge potential resale value. This helps in setting

a realistic purchase price.
4. **Future Potential:** Identify properties with untapped potential. Can you add square footage, create an open-concept layout, or enhance curb appeal?

Crunching Numbers: Estimating Costs and Potential Profits

Accurate financial analysis is crucial to determine potential profits and set budgets:

1. **Acquisition Costs:** Calculate the purchase price, closing costs, and any associated fees.
2. **Renovation Costs:** Estimate the cost of repairs, materials, labor, permits, and unforeseen contingencies.
3. **Carrying Costs:** Consider mortgage payments, property taxes, insurance, utilities, and other expenses while the property is being renovated.
4. **Resale Value:** Based on comparable sales and your renovations, project the property's potential resale value.
5. **Profit Margin:** Subtract all costs from the estimated resale value to calculate your potential profit. Aim for a margin that justifies the effort and risk.

Due Diligence: Evaluating the Property's Condition

Before finalizing a purchase, conduct thorough due diligence:

1. **Inspections:** Hire professionals to inspect the property's structure, electrical systems, plumbing, and more. Uncover hidden issues that might affect your budget.
2. **Permit Checks:** Ensure that past renovations were done with proper permits to avoid legal and financial complications.
3. **Title Search:** Verify the property's ownership history, any liens, and legal encumbrances that could affect your ability to resell.

4. **Zoning Regulations:** Confirm that the property complies with local zoning codes and regulations.

By mastering the art of real estate analysis, you'll be equipped to make informed decisions about which properties to pursue, how much to invest, and what potential profits to expect. In the next chapter, we'll explore the strategies and tactics for effectively negotiating deals and securing properties at favorable terms.

Chapter 4: Making Deals and Negotiations

Finding Properties: MLS, Auctions, Off-Market Deals, and More

To find potential flip-worthy properties, explore various sources:

1. **Multiple Listing Service (MLS):** Online platforms used by real estate agents to list properties for sale. MLS offers a wide range of properties.
2. **Auctions:** Attend foreclosure auctions, tax lien sales, or online auctions to find distressed properties at potentially lower prices.
3. **Off-Market Deals:** Network with real estate professionals, attend local real estate meetings, and use social media to uncover off-market opportunities.
4. **Direct Mail Campaigns:** Send targeted mail to homeowners who might be interested in selling, especially those with distressed properties.

Mastering the Art of Negotiation: Tips for Successful Deal-Making

Effective negotiation skills are crucial for securing favorable deals:

1. **Know Your Numbers:** Be well-versed in property values, renovation costs, and potential resale prices. This knowledge empowers you during negotiations.
2. **Build Rapport:** Establish a good rapport with sellers and their agents. A positive relationship can influence negotiations in your favor.
3. **Start with Research:** Research the seller's motivation, property history, and local market conditions before making an offer.

4. **Be Patient:** Don't rush negotiations. Be prepared to walk away from a deal if the terms aren't in your favor.
5. **Use Leverage:** Highlight your ability to close quickly and provide flexible terms. Leverage your financial readiness as a selling point.
6. **Offer Creative Solutions:** If a seller isn't willing to lower the price, propose other concessions such as a faster closing or covering certain fees.
7. **Multiple Offers:** In a competitive market, consider making multiple offers on different properties simultaneously to increase your chances of success.
8. **Counteroffers:** Be prepared for counteroffers and know your limits. Don't be afraid to negotiate until both parties are satisfied.

Due Diligence During Negotiations

1. **Inspection Contingency:** Include an inspection contingency in your offer to ensure you have the option to back out if significant issues are discovered.
2. **Financing Contingency:** Make your offer contingent on securing appropriate financing. This protects you if your funding falls through.
3. **Clear Communication:** Maintain clear and open communication with the seller or their agent throughout the negotiation process.

Building a Winning Offer

Craft an offer that balances your interests with the seller's needs:

1. **Purchase Price:** Propose a purchase price based on your research and budget. Aim for a price that allows for a comfortable profit margin.

2. **Contingencies:** Specify contingencies for inspections, financing, and other important factors.
3. **Closing Timeline:** Indicate a reasonable closing timeline that aligns with your project management schedule.
4. **Earnest Money Deposit:** Show your commitment by including an earnest money deposit with your offer.
5. **Seller Contributions:** Negotiate for the seller to cover certain closing costs or repairs.

Navigating negotiations requires finesse, research, and a strategic approach. By honing your negotiation skills, you increase your chances of securing properties at favorable terms and setting the stage for a successful house flipping venture. In the following chapter, we'll delve into the world of funding your flips and explore various financing options available to aspiring flippers.

Chapter 5: Funding Your Flips

Traditional Financing: Mortgages and Loans

Traditional financing options can provide stability and lower interest rates:

1. **Conventional Mortgage:** If you have a strong credit history, a conventional mortgage can offer competitive interest rates for purchasing a flip.
2. **FHA 203(k) Loan:** This government-backed loan combines the purchase price and renovation costs into a single mortgage, suitable for those needing extensive renovations.
3. **Home Equity Line of Credit (HELOC):** If you own a property with equity, a HELOC can provide funds for purchasing and renovating a flip.

Creative Financing: Private Lenders, Partnerships, and Hard Money Loans

Creative financing options can provide flexibility and quicker access to funds:

1. **Private Lenders:** Individuals or groups can lend you the necessary funds with negotiated terms, often quicker than traditional lenders.
2. **Partnerships:** Forming a partnership with someone who has the capital but lacks the time or expertise can be mutually beneficial.
3. **Hard Money Loans:** Short-term loans secured by the property, typically from private lenders. They have higher interest rates but can provide fast funding.

Calculating Risks: Managing Your Finances Responsibly

Mitigate financial risks by considering the following:

1. **Project Budget:** Create a comprehensive budget that includes acquisition costs, renovation expenses, carrying costs, and a contingency fund.
2. **Profit Margin:** Ensure your projected profit margin is sufficient to cover unexpected expenses and market fluctuations.
3. **Exit Strategy:** Have a backup plan if the property doesn't sell as quickly as expected. Can you rent it out temporarily to cover costs?
4. **Carrying Costs:** Calculate the costs of holding the property during renovations, including mortgage payments, property taxes, insurance, and utilities.
5. **Market Trends:** Keep an eye on market trends to adjust your pricing and strategies accordingly.

Risk Management: Setting Up Reserves

1. **Contingency Fund:** Allocate a percentage of your budget as a contingency fund to address unforeseen issues during renovations.
2. **Reserve Fund:** Maintain a reserve fund for covering ongoing carrying costs if your project takes longer than expected.
3. **Financial Cushion:** Have personal funds available to cover unexpected expenses if your project goes over budget.

Negotiating Financing Terms

1. **Interest Rates:** Negotiate favorable interest rates, especially when working with private lenders or hard money lenders.
2. **Terms and Repayment:** Clearly define repayment terms, whether it's monthly interest payments or a lump-sum

payment upon property sale.
3. **Collateral:** Understand what collateral the lender requires, which is typically the property you're purchasing.

Navigating the world of financing is essential for the success of your house flipping venture. By exploring traditional and creative financing options, calculating risks, and negotiating favorable terms, you'll be better equipped to secure the funds needed to acquire and renovate properties for profit. In the next chapter, we'll dive into the process of crafting a flawless renovation plan that maximizes the potential of your flip.

Chapter 6: Crafting a Flawless Renovation Plan

The Power of Curb Appeal: Enhancing Exterior Aesthetics

1. **Landscaping:** Improve the property's curb appeal with well-maintained lawns, shrubs, and flowers.
2. **Exterior Paint:** Fresh paint can transform the property's appearance. Choose neutral and modern colors.
3. **Roof and Siding:** Repair or replace damaged roofing and siding to ensure the property looks well-maintained.
4. **Windows and Doors:** Upgrade windows and doors for energy efficiency and a modern look.

Creating Functional Spaces: Kitchen, Bathroom, and Layout Considerations

1. **Kitchen:** Focus on updated appliances, modern cabinets, countertops, and lighting. A functional and attractive kitchen is a major selling point.
2. **Bathrooms:** Upgrade fixtures, tiles, and vanities. Consider adding extra storage and improving lighting.
3. **Open Layout:** If possible, create an open-concept layout to enhance the flow of the living spaces.
4. **Maximizing Space:** Utilize clever storage solutions to make the most of limited space.

Flooring, Paint, and Fixtures: Choosing Materials and Styles

1. **Flooring:** Opt for durable and attractive flooring materials like hardwood, laminate, or luxury vinyl.
2. **Paint:** Choose neutral colors for walls to appeal to a broad

range of buyers.
3. **Fixtures and Hardware:** Update light fixtures, faucets, doorknobs, and handles to add a modern touch.
4. **Consistency:** Maintain a consistent design style throughout the property to create a cohesive look.

DIY vs. Hiring Contractors: Pros, Cons, and Finding Reliable Professionals

1. **DIY Pros:** Cost savings and full control over design choices.
2. **DIY Cons:** Requires time, skills, and might lead to subpar workmanship.
3. **Contractor Pros:** Professional expertise, faster execution, and reduced stress.
4. **Contractor Cons:** Higher costs and reliance on external parties.

Project Management: Setting Timelines and Milestones

1. **Timeline:** Create a detailed project timeline that outlines when each task should be completed.
2. **Milestones:** Break the project into milestones to track progress and ensure deadlines are met.
3. **Flexibility:** Be prepared to adjust the timeline if unexpected delays occur.

Overcoming Common Challenges: Delays, Budget Overruns, and Unforeseen Issues

1. **Contingency Plan:** Allocate a contingency fund to address unexpected issues without derailing the project.
2. **Regular Inspections:** Conduct regular site inspections to identify issues early and make necessary adjustments.

3. **Communication:** Maintain open communication with contractors, suppliers, and team members to address challenges promptly.

The Importance of Quality Control: Inspections and Final Touches

1. **Inspections:** Thoroughly inspect completed work to ensure it meets quality standards and addresses any concerns.
2. **Final Walkthrough:** Conduct a comprehensive walkthrough to identify any remaining touch-ups or improvements.
3. **Attention to Detail:** Pay attention to small details that can make a big difference in the overall impression.

A well-crafted renovation plan is the foundation of a successful house flipping project. By focusing on curb appeal, functional spaces, quality materials, and efficient project management, you'll enhance the property's value and attract potential buyers. In the following chapter, we'll delve into the process of effectively marketing and selling your flip to maximize profits.

Chapter 7: Executing the Flip

Project Management: Setting Timelines and Milestones

1. **Detailed Timeline:** Stick to the established project timeline to ensure renovations are completed efficiently.
2. **Milestone Tracking:** Monitor progress by tracking milestones, such as completion of specific rooms or major tasks.
3. **Communication:** Maintain open communication with contractors, suppliers, and team members to address any delays promptly.

Overcoming Common Challenges: Delays, Budget Overruns, and Unforeseen Issues

1. **Contingency Plan:** Utilize the contingency fund to address unexpected issues without compromising the budget.
2. **Budget Monitoring:** Keep a close eye on expenses to prevent budget overruns. Adjust spending if necessary.
3. **Problem Solving:** Address challenges such as supply shortages or unexpected complications with a proactive approach.

Quality Control and Final Touches

1. **Inspections:** Regularly inspect the progress to ensure the work meets your standards and adheres to the renovation plan.
2. **Attention to Detail:** Focus on final touches that enhance the property's overall appeal, such as clean lines and consistent aesthetics.
3. **Finishing On Time:** Prioritize tasks that can impact the project's completion date, such as final paint, flooring, and fixture installations.

Preparing for Marketing and Sale

1. **Staging for Success:** Stage the property to showcase its potential. Arrange furniture and decor to create a welcoming and appealing atmosphere.
2. **Professional Photography:** Invest in high-quality photography to capture the property's best features and attract online buyers.
3. **Compelling Listings:** Write engaging property descriptions that highlight its unique qualities, location benefits, and renovation details.
4. **Pricing Strategy:** Research comparable sales in the area and set a competitive price that aligns with current market trends.

Hosting Open Houses: Attracting Potential Buyers

1. **Event Planning:** Organize well-advertised open houses to attract a larger pool of potential buyers.
2. **Prepare the Property:** Ensure the property is clean, well-lit, and properly staged before hosting an open house.
3. **Engage Visitors:** Interact with visitors, answer their questions, and provide information about the property's features and renovations.

Negotiating Offers and Closing the Deal

1. **Reviewing Offers:** Evaluate offers based on the proposed terms, price, and the buyer's financial readiness.
2. **Counteroffers:** If necessary, make counteroffers that align with your desired terms while keeping negotiations respectful.
3. **Due Diligence:** Work with your real estate agent to ensure all necessary documents are completed and the transaction progresses smoothly.

Handing Over the Keys: A Successful Sale

1. **Final Inspections:** Address any inspection-related issues and ensure the property meets all contractual obligations.
2. **Closing Process:** Work with your real estate agent and legal professionals to navigate the closing process, including paperwork and fund transfers.
3. **Celebrate Success:** Celebrate the successful sale and the culmination of your hard work and strategic planning.

Executing a house flip requires careful management, attention to detail, and effective communication. By following the steps outlined in this chapter, you'll be well-prepared to carry out a successful renovation and market your property to potential buyers. In the next chapter, we'll delve into the process of evaluating your flip's financial outcome and learning from the experience.

Chapter 8: Marketing and Selling Your Flip

Staging for Success: Showcasing the Property's Potential

1. **Neutral Decor:** Opt for neutral colors and decor that appeals to a broad range of buyers.
2. **Furniture Arrangement:** Arrange furniture to create a sense of space and flow. Highlight the property's best features.
3. **Declutter:** Remove personal items and excess clutter to make rooms feel larger and more inviting.
4. **Curb Appeal:** Ensure the exterior is well-maintained, with trimmed lawns, clean walkways, and inviting landscaping.

Crafting Compelling Listings: Descriptions and High-Quality Photography

1. **Captivating Descriptions:** Write descriptions that highlight the property's unique features, renovations, and lifestyle benefits.
2. **Professional Photography:** Invest in professional photography to capture the property's best angles and showcase its transformation.
3. **Virtual Tours:** Offer virtual tours to provide potential buyers with an immersive experience of the property.

Pricing Strategies: Finding the Sweet Spot for Maximum Profit

1. **Comparative Market Analysis (CMA):** Conduct a CMA to analyze recent sales of comparable properties and determine a competitive price.
2. **Positioning:** Price your property slightly below the market

average to attract more attention and potentially spark bidding wars.
3. **Competitive Pricing:** Set a price that reflects the property's value and the renovations you've undertaken.

Hosting Open Houses: Attracting Potential Buyers

1. **Event Planning:** Plan open houses on weekends when more potential buyers are available. Advertise them through various channels.
2. **Warm Welcome:** Create a welcoming atmosphere with refreshments and music. Allow visitors to explore the property at their own pace.
3. **Engage:** Be available to answer questions, highlight renovations, and address any concerns visitors may have.

Digital Marketing: Reaching a Wider Audience

1. **Online Listings:** Advertise your property on real estate websites, ensuring high-quality photos and a compelling description.
2. **Social Media:** Utilize platforms like Instagram, Facebook, and LinkedIn to showcase before-and-after photos and engage with potential buyers.
3. **Email Marketing:** Send property listings to your network and subscribers to spread the word about your flip.

Negotiating Offers and Closing the Deal

1. **Prompt Responses:** Respond quickly to inquiries and offers to maintain interest and momentum.
2. **Multiple Offers:** If you receive multiple offers, carefully evaluate each one and consider asking for best and final offers.

3. **Terms and Conditions:** Review offers for terms beyond the sale price, such as financing contingencies and proposed closing dates.

Post-Sale Analysis and Learning

1. **Evaluating Profit:** Compare the final sale price with your initial projections to determine the actual profit.
2. **Learning from Experience:** Reflect on the project, identifying successes and areas for improvement in your future flips.
3. **Continuous Learning:** Stay updated on market trends, buyer preferences, and renovation techniques for ongoing success.

Selling your flip requires strategic marketing, effective communication, and negotiation skills. By implementing the strategies outlined in this chapter, you'll increase your chances of attracting interested buyers and securing a successful sale. In the next chapter, we'll explore the intricacies of the closing process and the final steps to complete a house flip.

Chapter 9: Closing the Deal

Navigating the Closing Process: Paperwork and Legalities

1. **Purchase Agreement Review:** Work closely with your real estate agent to review the purchase agreement, ensuring all terms are accurate.
2. **Title Search and Insurance:** Conduct a thorough title search to ensure there are no liens or ownership disputes. Obtain title insurance to protect against potential issues.
3. **Inspections and Repairs:** Address any inspection-related issues, negotiate repairs if necessary, and provide documentation of completed work.

Dealing with Appraisals and Inspections

1. **Appraisal Process:** The buyer's lender will likely order an appraisal to ensure the property's value matches the sale price. Be prepared to provide documentation on renovations.
2. **Inspection Resolution:** If any issues arise during the buyer's inspection, negotiate solutions or repairs to move the process forward.

Handing Over the Keys: A Successful Sale

1. **Final Walkthrough:** Conduct a final walkthrough with the buyer to ensure the property is in the agreed-upon condition.
2. **Transfer of Ownership:** Complete necessary paperwork to transfer ownership, including the deed, transfer tax forms, and other legal documents.
3. **Funds Transfer:** Coordinate with the escrow company to ensure a smooth transfer of funds from the buyer's lender to

your account.

Completing the Closing Process: Celebrating Success

1. **Closing Statement Review:** Review the closing statement to ensure all financial details are accurate, including credits, prorations, and fees.
2. **Signing Documents:** Sign the necessary closing documents, which may include the deed, bill of sale, and any other required paperwork.
3. **Celebrate the Success:** Celebrate the completion of your house flip and the successful sale of the property.

Transitioning to New Ventures: Long-Term Real Estate Wealth

1. **Assessing Your Next Move:** Decide whether you'll reinvest your profits into new flips, expand your real estate portfolio, or explore other investment opportunities.
2. **Rental Properties:** Consider the option of converting future flips into rental properties to generate a steady stream of passive income.
3. **Continued Learning:** Stay informed about market trends and opportunities for ongoing success in real estate.

The closing process marks the culmination of your house flipping journey. By navigating the legalities, ensuring a smooth transition of ownership, and celebrating your success, you'll conclude your flip on a high note. In the final chapter, we'll discuss the importance of continuous learning, adapting to market trends, and growing your house flipping business.

Chapter 10: Learning and Growing

Evaluating Your Flip: Post-Project Analysis

1. **Financial Assessment:** Compare your projected profits with the actual outcome to identify areas of success and improvement.
2. **Timeline Analysis:** Evaluate whether the project was completed within the planned timeline and identify any delays.
3. **Renovation Review:** Assess the quality of renovations and gather feedback from buyers to understand their preferences.

Continuous Learning: Adapting to Market Trends and Changes

1. **Stay Informed:** Keep up with real estate market trends, economic shifts, and buyer preferences to make informed decisions.
2. **Networking:** Attend real estate seminars, workshops, and conferences to connect with industry professionals and gain insights.
3. **Reading and Research:** Regularly read books, articles, and reports on real estate investing to expand your knowledge.

Scaling Up: Growing Your House Flipping Business

1. **Refine Strategies:** Apply lessons learned from previous flips to refine your strategies for future projects.
2. **Building a Team:** As your business grows, consider building a reliable team of contractors, agents, and financial partners.
3. **Diversification:** Explore opportunities beyond single-family home flips, such as multi-unit properties or commercial real estate.

Risk Management: Maintaining a Balanced Approach

1. **Assess Risk Tolerance:** Regularly reassess your risk tolerance and adjust your strategies accordingly.
2. **Financial Prudence:** Ensure you maintain a healthy financial cushion to handle unexpected challenges.
3. **Learning from Setbacks:** Embrace setbacks as learning experiences and use them to strengthen your future endeavors.

Contributing to the Real Estate Community

1. **Mentorship:** Share your experiences with aspiring flippers and offer guidance to help them navigate the challenges.
2. **Educational Initiatives:** Contribute articles, videos, or presentations to provide valuable insights to the real estate community.
3. **Giving Back:** Consider philanthropic initiatives related to housing, real estate education, or community development.

By continually learning and adapting, you can position yourself for long-term success in the house flipping industry. Embrace change, refine your strategies, and stay connected with fellow real estate professionals to grow your business and make a positive impact on the industry as a whole.

Chapter 11: Pitfalls to Avoid

Overestimating Potential Profits

1. **Solution:** Conduct thorough research to accurately estimate renovation costs, resale value, and potential expenses.

Underestimating Renovation Costs

1. **Solution:** Obtain multiple quotes from contractors, factor in contingencies, and be prepared for unexpected expenses.

Skipping Due Diligence

1. **Solution:** Perform thorough inspections, review property history, and confirm zoning regulations to avoid legal and structural issues.

Neglecting Market Research

1. **Solution:** Stay informed about local market trends, demand, and neighborhood dynamics to make informed decisions.

Ignoring Project Management

1. **Solution:** Develop a detailed project timeline, communicate effectively with contractors, and monitor progress closely.

Choosing the Wrong Location

1. **Solution:** Research neighborhoods carefully, considering factors like school quality, amenities, and potential for growth.

Overpaying for Properties

1. **Solution:** Stick to your budget and avoid emotional decisions. Be prepared to walk away from deals that don't align with your financial goals.

Poor Negotiation Skills

1. **Solution:** Develop strong negotiation skills and be prepared to negotiate terms that benefit both parties.

Inadequate Financing Planning

1. **Solution:** Secure financing before making offers, create a comprehensive budget, and have a contingency fund for unexpected expenses.

Underestimating Carrying Costs

1. **Solution:** Account for mortgage payments, property taxes, insurance, and utilities during the renovation period.

Over-Improving the Property

1. **Solution:** Focus on renovations that align with the neighborhood and potential buyer preferences, avoiding excessive upgrades that won't yield a higher return.

Rushing the Sale Process

1. **Solution:** Be patient and wait for the right buyer who appreciates the property's value and renovations.

Lack of Flexibility

1. **Solution:** Stay adaptable to changing market conditions and be prepared to adjust your strategies as needed.

Not Learning from Mistakes

1. **Solution:** Analyze failures and setbacks, and use them as learning opportunities to improve future projects.

Inadequate Exit Strategy

1. **Solution:** Plan for alternative scenarios, such as renting the property if it doesn't sell quickly, to minimize financial risks.

By recognizing and avoiding these common pitfalls, you'll increase your chances of success in the house flipping industry. Continuously educate yourself, plan meticulously, and adapt to challenges to create a sustainable and profitable house flipping business.

Chapter 12: Case Studies: Real-Life Flipping Examples

Case Study 1: The Renovation Triumph

Challenge: The property was in a state of disrepair, requiring extensive renovations.

Strategy: The investor created a comprehensive renovation plan, focusing on modernizing the interior while enhancing curb appeal.

Outcome: After meticulous renovations, the property sold quickly at a significant profit due to the stunning transformation and desirable location.

Key Takeaway: Thorough planning and strategic renovations can lead to substantial profits even when dealing with heavily distressed properties.

Case Study 2: Location, Location, Location

Challenge: The property was in a desirable location but needed updates to match buyer expectations.

Strategy: The investor focused on cosmetic improvements, modernizing the interior design, and enhancing curb appeal.

Outcome: With minimal renovation expenses, the property sold above the initial purchase price due to its prime location and updated look.

Key Takeaway: Leveraging a property's location and making targeted improvements can yield impressive returns with less extensive renovations.

Case Study 3: The Unforeseen Obstacles

Challenge: Unexpected structural issues were discovered during the renovation, causing delays and increased expenses.

Strategy: The investor quickly addressed the structural issues and adjusted the renovation plan to maintain the property's appeal.

Outcome: Despite setbacks, the property sold with a modest profit due to the investor's ability to adapt and resolve challenges.

Key Takeaway: Being prepared for unexpected obstacles and having a flexible approach to project management is crucial for navigating unforeseen issues.

Case Study 4: Market Timing Matters

Challenge: The property was in good condition, but it was listed during a slow market period.

Strategy: The investor focused on competitive pricing, staged the property effectively, and targeted marketing efforts.

Outcome: By waiting for the market to improve slightly and strategically pricing the property, it sold with a reasonable profit.

Key Takeaway: Timing the sale to align with favorable market conditions and using effective marketing strategies can impact the final profit.

Case Study 5: The Power of Collaboration

Challenge: The investor lacked the necessary construction skills to handle extensive renovations.

Strategy: The investor formed a partnership with a contractor, leveraging each other's strengths to efficiently complete the project.

Outcome: The property was renovated and sold successfully, demonstrating the benefits of collaboration in the flipping process.

Key Takeaway: Building partnerships with professionals can help overcome skill gaps and enhance the overall success of a flip.

These case studies showcase the diverse challenges and strategies involved in house flipping. From strategic renovations to location advantages, flexibility in handling unexpected issues, market timing, and collaborative efforts, each example illustrates valuable lessons for aspiring house flippers. By studying real-life scenarios, you can gain insights that will contribute to your success in the industry.

Chapter 13: Beyond Flipping: Long-Term Real Estate Wealth

Exploring Long-Term Investment Strategies

1. **Rental Properties:** Consider purchasing properties to rent out, generating consistent passive income over time.
2. **Multi-Unit Properties:** Investing in multi-unit properties can provide multiple income streams and potentially higher returns.
3. **Commercial Real Estate:** Explore opportunities in commercial real estate, such as retail or office spaces, for diversified investments.

Benefits of Long-Term Investments

1. **Steady Income:** Rental properties offer reliable monthly income, helping you build wealth over time.
2. **Appreciation:** Real estate tends to appreciate in value over the long term, increasing your overall net worth.
3. **Tax Advantages:** Real estate investments come with tax benefits, including deductions for mortgage interest and property expenses.

Risk Management and Portfolio Diversification

1. **Diversify Asset Types:** Balance your portfolio with different types of real estate investments to spread risk.
2. **Market Exposure:** Invest in various markets to reduce the impact of localized economic downturns.

Property Management and Passive Income

1. **Hiring Property Managers:** As your portfolio grows, consider hiring property managers to handle day-to-day operations.
2. **Passive Income:** Rental income can provide a steady source of passive income, freeing you from constant hands-on involvement.

Leveraging Financing Strategies

1. **Leverage Equity:** Use the equity from your flips to finance rental property acquisitions.
2. **Creative Financing:** Explore options like seller financing, private lenders, and partnerships for funding.

Real Estate Syndication and Investment Groups

1. **Real Estate Syndication:** Join real estate syndication deals to invest in larger properties and access opportunities you might not have individually.
2. **Investment Groups:** Join local real estate investment groups to network, learn, and potentially collaborate on deals.

Long-Term Wealth Building Mindset

1. **Patience:** Long-term real estate wealth requires patience and a focus on sustained growth.
2. **Educational Continuity:** Stay informed about market trends, investment strategies, and legal changes affecting real estate.
3. **Adaptability:** Be open to adjusting your strategies based on changing market conditions and economic trends.

Beyond flipping, long-term real estate investment offers a path to financial stability and wealth accumulation. By strategically diversifying your portfolio, leveraging financing, and exploring passive income opportunities, you can build a sustainable real estate business that generates consistent income and appreciates over time. This chapter concludes your journey through the world of house flipping and real estate investment. Remember, success comes with continuous learning, adaptability, and a commitment to making informed decisions.

Appendix

Resources for Aspiring House Flippers and Real Estate Investors:

1. Real Estate Books:
    - "The Book on Flipping Houses" by J. Scott
    - "The Millionaire Real Estate Investor" by Gary Keller
    - "The ABCs of Real Estate Investing" by Ken McElroy
2. Online Platforms:
    - Multiple Listing Service (MLS) websites for property listings.
    - Real estate forums and communities for networking and learning.
    - Real estate investment websites offering educational content and resources.
3. Real Estate Seminars and Workshops:
    - Attend local or online seminars and workshops to learn from experienced investors and industry experts.
4. Property Analysis Tools:
    - Real estate analysis software to evaluate potential deals, estimate renovation costs, and calculate potential profits.
5. Real Estate Investment Clubs:
    - Join local real estate investment clubs to network, share experiences, and learn from fellow investors.
6. Mentorship and Coaching:
    - Seek mentorship from experienced flippers or real estate professionals to receive personalized guidance.
7. Online Courses:
    - Enroll in online courses covering topics such as real estate investment strategies, property analysis, and renovation.

8. Legal and Financial Advisors:
    - Consult with real estate attorneys, accountants, and financial advisors to ensure your investments are legally and financially sound.

Glossary of Terms:

- **ARV (After Repair Value):** The estimated value of a property after it has been renovated.
- **Contingency Fund:** An allocated amount of money set aside to cover unforeseen expenses during a project.
- **CMA (Comparative Market Analysis):** An evaluation of comparable properties in a specific area to determine a property's market value.
- **Hard Money Loan:** A short-term, high-interest loan secured by the property being purchased or renovated.
- **HELOC (Home Equity Line of Credit):** A line of credit secured by the equity in a property, which can be used for various purposes.
- **MLS (Multiple Listing Service):** An online platform used by real estate agents to list properties for sale.
- **Private Lender:** An individual or group that lends money for real estate investments.
- **ROI (Return on Investment):** A measure of the profitability of an investment, calculated as a percentage of the initial investment.
- **Title Insurance:** An insurance policy that protects against financial loss due to title defects or ownership disputes.
- **Wholesaling:** The practice of finding properties at a discount and then selling them to other investors without performing renovations.

Legal Disclaimer:

This book provides general information about house flipping and real estate investment. It is not intended as professional advice and should not be considered a substitute for consulting with qualified legal, financial, or real estate professionals. The author and publisher are not liable for any losses or damages resulting from decisions made based on the information provided in this book.

Acknowledgments:

The author would like to express gratitude to all the real estate professionals, mentors, and colleagues whose insights and experiences have contributed to the content of this book. Their expertise has been invaluable in shaping the guidance provided to aspiring house flippers and real estate investors.

www.ingramcontent.com/pod-product-compliance
Lightning Source LLC
LaVergne TN
LVHW092101060526
838201LV00047B/1508